GETTING TO KNOW THE WORLD'S GREATEST ARTISTS

GEORGES
SEURAT

WRITTEN AND ILLUSTRATED BY MIKE VENEZIA

CHILDREN'S PRESS®
A DIVISION OF SCHOLASTIC INC.
NEW YORK TORONTO LONDON AUCKLAND SYDNEY
MEXICO CITY NEW DELHI HONG KONG
DANBURY, CONNECTICUT

Cover: *Sunday Afternoon on the Island of La Grande Jatte,* by Georges Seurat. 1884, oil on canvas, 207.6 x 308 cm. © Art Institute of Chicago, Helen Birch Bartlett Memorial Collection, 1926.224.

Colorist for illustrations: Dave Ludwig

Library of Congress Cataloging-in-Publication Data

Venezia, Mike.
  Georges Seurat / written and illustrated by Mike Venezia.
     p. cm. — (Getting to know the world's greatest artists)
Summary: Describes the life and career of the nineteenth-century French
Neo-Impressionist artist Georges Seurat, best known for inventing the
painting technique known as Pointillism.
  ISBN 0-516-22496-4 (lib. bdg.)   0-516-27813-4 (pbk.)
  1. Seurat, Georges, 1859-1891—Juvenile literature. 2.
Artists—France—Biography—Juvenile literature. 3. Neo-impressionism
(Art)—France—Juvenile literature. [1. Seurat, Georges, 1859-1891. 2.
Artists.] I. Seurat, Georges, 1859-1891. II. Title.
  N6853.S48 V46 2002
  759.4—dc21

                  2002001609

CHILDREN'S PRESS and associated logos are trademarks and or
registered trademarks of Grolier Publishing Co., Inc.
SCHOLASTIC and associated logos are trademarks and or
registered trademarks of Scholastic Inc.

16 17 18 19 20 21 22 R 21 20   62

Georges Seurat, by Ernest J. Laurent. pencil on paper. © Art Resource, NY, Réunion des Musées Nationaux, photo by C. Jean.

Georges Seurat was born in Paris, France, in 1859. At that time, Paris was the art center of the world. As a young man, Georges worked very hard to find a new way of painting that had never been seen before.

Invitation to the Sideshow, by Georges Seurat. 1887-1888, oil on canvas, 99.7 x 149.9 cm.
© Metropolitan Museum of Art, Bequest of Stephen C. Clark, 1960, (61.101.17).

To make his paintings look different and
fresh, Georges Seurat used scientific ideas
he discovered about color, line, and shapes.

Some of Georges's beautifully designed paintings seem to shimmer and glow with light. Others have the feeling of a hot, misty, summer day.

The Channel of Gravelines, Petit Fort Philippe, by Georges Seurat. 1890, oil on canvas, 36 x 43 7/8 in.
© Indianapolis Museum of Art, Gift of Mrs. James W. Fesler in memory of Daniel W. and Elizabeth C. Marmon.

Sunday Afternoon on the Island of La Grande Jatte (detail), by Georges Seurat. 1884, oil on canvas, 207.6 x 308 cm. © Art Institute of Chicago, Helen Birch Bartlett Memorial Collection, 1926.224, detail #25.

Georges Seurat is probably best known for inventing Pointillism. Pointillism was Georges's method of putting little dots and touches of different colors of paint next to each other. Instead of mixing up red and yellow paint to make orange, for instance, Georges would put dots of red and yellow next to each other.

Invitation to the Sideshow (detail #3), by Georges Seurat. 1887-1888, oil on canvas, 99.7 x 149.9 cm. © Metropolitan Museum of Art, Bequest of Stephen C. Clark, 1960, (61.101.17) detail #3.

That way, your eye would mix the color right on the canvas. Georges Seurat believed this method would make his colors appear more natural and real looking—almost like colored light!

Le Chahut, by Georges Seurat. 1889-1890, oil on canvas, 66 1/8 x 55 1/2 in. © Art Resource, NY, Rijksmuseum Kroller-Muller, Otterlo, Netherlands, photo by Erich Lessing.

Georges also discovered that the way he put lines and shapes in a painting could give the viewer a feeling of being happy, or calm, or sad.

In *Le Chahut,* the dancers' legs and positions of the musicians' arms and instruments are all pointing upwards, to create a happy, fun feeling. In the painting below, the horizontal lines and shapes of the sandy shore and horizon give a feeling of a quiet, calm, relaxed, day.

Channel of Gravelines, Grand Fort-Philippe, by Georges Seurat. 1890, oil on canvas, 65 x 81 cm.
© National Gallery, London.

The scientific ideas Georges studied about and used in his paintings are called theories. Georges learned about these theories in books that had just been published at the time. Scientific discoveries were being made all over Europe in the 1880s. Every day, Europeans were learning more about medicine, photography, mechanics, chemistry–just about everything–including art!

11

Georges Seurat grew up in a rather unusual home. His father preferred to live by himself a few miles outside of Paris. He visited his family only once in a while for dinner.

Mr. Seurat had lost his arm in a hunting accident years before. He invented a device that allowed him to attach knives and forks onto the end of his arm.

Georges's father was proud to be able to carve and serve a whole dinner roast at lightning speed. Sometimes dinner guests were surprised. One guest was probably Georges's best friend, Édmond-François Aman-Jean. Both Aman-Jean and Georges were interested in being artists. They ended up going to the same art school together.

The Phrygian Sibyl, by Raphael. chalk.
© Ashmolean Museum, Oxford, Western
Art Department.

Arab Horses Fighting in a Stable, by Eugéne Delacroix. 1860, oil on canvas,
64.6 x 81 cm. © Art Resource, NY, Réunion des Musées Nationaux,
Louvre, Paris, photo by Gerard Blot.

In 1878, Seurat and his friend Aman-Jean entered the best-known art school in Paris, the École des Beaux-Arts. At this school, students learned by copying statues and paintings done by great artists from the past.

Portrait of Mme Louise-Nicolas-Marie Destouches, by Jean
Auguste Dominique Ingres. 1816, graphite, 39.5 x 28 cm.
© Art Resource, NY, Réunion des Musées Nationaux,
photo by J.G. Berizzi.

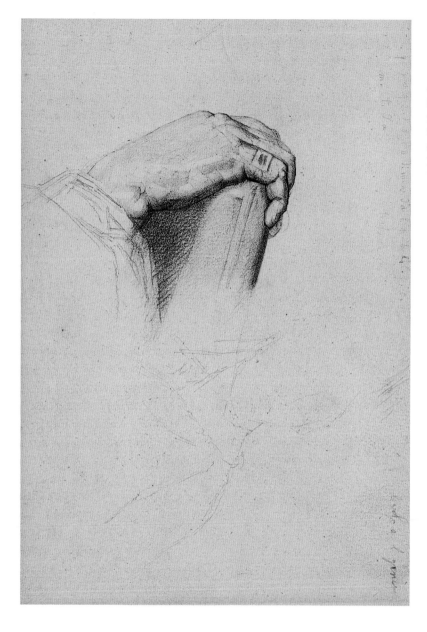

Georges found plenty of great works of art in Paris. Among his favorites were the paintings of Italian Renaissance artist Raphael and early 19th-century French artists J. A. D. Ingres and Eugéne Delacroix.

Before the Balcony,
by Georges Seurat.
pencil, 31 x 24 cm.
© Art Resource,
NY, Réunion des
Musées Nationaux,
Louvre, Paris.

It didn't take long for Georges Seurat to get tired of copying other artists' work, though. Soon Georges stopped going to his art classes. He began spending more time thinking about how to make works of art that were really original and all his own.

Ploughing, by Georges Seurat. pencil, 27.5 x 32 cm.
© Art Resource, NY, Réunion des Musées Nationaux, Louvre, Paris.

In 1881, when Georges Seurat was 22 years old, he set up a studio and began to follow his dream by creating wonderful drawings. In these drawings, Georges explored the importance of shapes and form. He used a smeary graphite-and-clay crayon (called a conté crayon) on bumpy paper. Even though these drawings are black and white, they seem to sparkle with light.

Farm Women at Work, by Georges Seurat. 1882-1883, oil on canvas, 38.5 x 46.2 cm.
© Solomon R. Guggenheim Museum, New York, Gift, Solomon R. Guggenheim, 1941,
photo by David Heald.

While Georges was working on his drawings,
he began experimenting with color.

Georges made lots of small paintings. He learned that by using criss-cross brush strokes that went every which way, his paintings would appear to shimmer with light.

Seated Woman, by Georges Seurat. 1883, oil on canvas, 38.1 x 46.2 cm.
© Solomon R. Guggenheim Museum, New York, Gift, Solomon R. Guggenheim, 1937,
photo by David Heald.

Garden, Spring and Flowers, Spring at Pontoise, by Camille Pissarro. 1877, oil on canvas, 65.5 x 81 cm. © Art Resource, NY, Réunion des Musées Nationaux, Musee d'Orsay, Paris, photo by Herve Lewandowski.

Woman with Parasol turned to the Left, by Claude Monet. 1886, oil on canvas, 131 x 88 cm. © Bridgeman Art Library International Ltd. London/New York, Musee d'Orsay, Paris, France, photo by Peter Will.

Dance at Bougival, by Pierre Auguste Renoir. 1882-1883, oil on canvas, 182 x 98 cm. © Bridgeman Art Library International Ltd., London/New York, Museum of Fine Arts, Boston, MA.

One day, Georges and some friends saw the work of the Impressionist artists at an art show. The paintings of Impressionist artists Claude Monet, Alfred Sisley, Camille Pissarro, and Pierre Auguste Renoir were the talk of Paris in the 1880s.

These artists were interested in capturing a moment in time of a happy, everyday scene. They worked outdoors, quickly brushing colorful flecks of paint onto their canvases. Even though their paintings were quite colorful, Georges Seurat thought he could do better.

Study for Une Baignade, Asnières, by Georges Seurat. 1883, oil on canvas, 17.45 x 26.34 cm.
© Nelson-Atkins Museum of Art, Kansas City, MO, Purchase: Nelson Trust, photo by Mel McLean, 33-15/3.

In 1883, Georges felt ready to begin his first important painting. It was called *Une Baignade, Asnières (Bathers at Asnières)*. Georges chose a happy, everyday scene, but went about painting it much differently than the Impressionists would have.

Georges worked much more slowly. During the day, he went to the riverside and made lots of drawings and color sketches. He then brought them back to his studio and worked

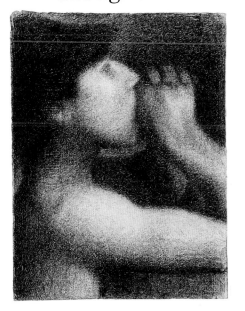

late into the night, carefully placing each figure onto his large canvas. Georges's finished painting was almost 6 feet (1.8 meters) high and 10 feet (3 m) wide!

L'Echo, Study for Une Baignade, Asnières, by Georges Seurat.

Une Baignade, Asnières (Bathers at Asnières), by Georges Seurat. 1884, oil on canvas, 201 x 300 cm.
© Bridgeman Art Library International Ltd., London/New York, National Gallery, London, UK.

Georges Seurat spent more than a year working on his large painting. *Bathers at Asnières* was exhibited at a new art show that Georges and his friends helped set up. It was called the Salon des Indépendants Artists.

This was an important time for Georges Seurat. Not only did his painting get a lot of attention, but Georges met and made friends with artists who would help him form a new art group known as the Neo-Impressionists.

Georges's new friends all liked his scientific ideas about color and composition. They often met at cafés to discuss their feelings about art. Soon Georges became the group's leader. Georges's artist friends admired him so much that they started dressing like him. They trimmed their beards like Georges's and even wore their hats the same way.

Study for Sunday Afternoon on the Island of La Grande Jatte, by Georges Seurat. 1884/1885, oil on wood, 15.9 x 25 cm. © National Gallery of Art, Washington, DC, Ailsa Mellon Bruce Collection.

Georges Seurat soon began his next large painting. It was a scene of a small island where hardworking Parisians went to relax on the weekend.

Georges worked the same way as he had before. He made dozens of color sketches during the day, brought them back to his studio, and worked late into the night by the light of a kerosene lamp.

Oil sketch for Sunday Afternoon on the Island of La Grande Jatte, by Georges Seurat. 1884, oil on panel, 15.5 x 25.1 cm. © Art Institute of Chicago, Gift of Mary and Leigh Block, 1981.15.

After two years, Georges Seurat finished his greatest masterpiece, *Sunday Afternoon on the Island of La Grande Jatte.* It was the first

Sunday Afternoon on the Island of La Grande Jatte, by Georges Seurat. 1884, oil on canvas, 207.6 x 308 cm. © Art Institute of Chicago, Helen Birch Bartlett Memorial Collection, 1926.224.

time Georges used Pointillism over the entire surface of a painting.

Sunday Afternoon on the Island of La Grande Jatte is very large, too. If you get a chance to see it in person, you'll be amazed by what happens when you step back a few feet from the painting. The warm, sunny dots and cool, shady dots of color mix together to create new colors right before your eyes!

When *Sunday Afternoon on the Island of La Grande Jatte* was first shown, many people liked it, but some critics thought Georges's figures looked too stiff. They thought scientific theories about color and composition had no place in art and could make a painting look like it was made by a machine.

At the Concert Européen, by Georges Seurat. 1887-88, conté crayon on paper, 31.1 x 23.9 cm. © Museum of Modern Art, New York, Lillie P. Bliss Collection.

Georges Seurat never listened to his critics. He knew that *Sunday Afternoon on the Island of La Grande Jatte* captured the feeling of a beautiful and endless summer day that shimmered with warm sunlight.

Georges Seurat went on to make drawings and Pointillism paintings of all kinds of scenes. Some of his favorites were of the concerts, music halls, and circuses he loved attending.

Le Cirque, by Georges Seurat. 1890-1891, oil on canvas, 73 x 59 1/8 in. © Art Resource, NY, Musee d'Orsay, Paris, France, photo by Erich Lessing.

Port-en-Bessin, by Georges Seurat.
1888, oil on canvas, 25 1/2 x 32 1/2 in.
© Minneapolis Institute of Arts,
The William Hood Dunwitty Fund.

Sometimes Georges would travel to small seaport villages and relax by painting peaceful scenes of boats and harbors. Georges Seurat probably worked hardest on the colors in his paintings. Sometimes he would paint a Pointillism border, or even a whole frame, to make sure his picture was surrounded by exactly the right colors.

View of Le Crotoy, from Upstream,
by Georges Seurat. 1889, oil on canvas,
70.5 x 86.7 cm. © Bridgeman Art
Library International Ltd., London/New
York, Detroit Institute of Arts, USA,
Bequest of Robert H. Tannahill.

Young Woman Powdering Herself, by Georges Seurat. 1889, oil on canvas, 25.7 x 16.8 cm. © Bridgeman Art Library International Ltd., London/New York, Museum of Fine Arts, Houston, TX, USA, Gift of Audrey Jones Beck.

Georges Seurat got sick and died suddenly in 1891. He lived to be only 32 years old. In a few short years, he created a remarkable art style. Georges Seurat influenced many other famous artists of the time, including Vincent Van Gogh, Paul Gauguin, Henri de Toulouse-Lautrec, and Henri Matisse. All of these great artists tried versions of Pointillism in their own paintings.

Works of art in this book can be seen at the following places:

Art Institute of Chicago
Ashmolean Museum, Oxford
Detroit Institute of Arts
Indianapolis Museum of Art
Louvre, Paris
Metropolitan Museum of Art, New York
Minneapolis Institute of Arts
Musee d'Orsay, Paris
Museum of Fine Arts, Boston
Museum of Fine Arts, Houston
Museum of Modern Art, New York

National Gallery, London
National Gallery of Art,
   Washington, D.C.
Nelson-Atkins Museum of Art,
   Kansas City
Réunion des Musées Nationaux, Paris
Rijksmuseum Kroller-Muller, Otterlo
Solomon R. Guggenheim Museum,
   New York
Yale University Art Gallery, New Haven